invaluable
LESSONS

SME Business Management Tips

SUKUMAR BERA

Invaluable Lessons

Made with ❤ on the Notion Press Platform

www.notionpress.com

Dedicated to any self-inspired person who aspires to achieve SME business success

Contents

Foreword

In the course of managing the business and dealing with different individuals I often encounter with a wide array of questions, problems and situations that demands a holistic solution.

At times business friends finds their business advisor in me and get their queries resolved with my few suggestions.

I consider this to be *gift from the divine* that interesting ideas and solutions come to me that helped hundreds of my dealer friends, company executives and others and on the top of it, it scaled-up my business to a great level that I could have ever imagined in my business carrier.

For the sake of all those who is carrying forward SMEs, in the best of their capacity, I have poured in all the ideas, working style and thinking style that can help them to sail over business problems and may take their business growth to a decent height.

The ideas given on this book are purely based on my experiences, principles, mistakes all throughout these years.

Kindly do not consider this book as the only means to business success. Have an all-encompassing mind, ready to learn from all corners of the world.

Still this book can serve you as a guide to not commit those mistakes which are not so congenial for business growth.

Best Wishes!

Mr Sukumar Bera,

Managing Director,
Bera Distributors Pvt. Ltd.
Midnapore, 721101
West Bengal, India

Acknowledgments

I shall take a moment to thank my son, Shiv Kumar Bera for crafting the book, starting from designing, drafting, writing, printing and publishing to both offline and online platforms like Amazon & Flipkart.

I shall also thank to all dear readers, my dealer friends, company executives, representatives whose quest of asking questions, and appetite to learn has made to compose this book.

Respect All, Trust None

This forms part of your *thinking style.*

Particularly while into business, dealing with business activities never ever assume anything and never ever put blind faith on anybody.

Cross check multiple times, cross-verify multiple times if possible and then go ahead.

For example,

You have asked your employee to complete a task of *key importance* within certain time. And you happen to be on a vacation for some days during that time.

So never assume that task shall be done perfectly by that time. It's good if it is done so.

But always keep an eye whether it's done and whether it's done perfectly or not.

Yes, it's not always possible to keep an eye on each and every task being designated but at least on certain confidential tasks, tasks of key importance for the company or the organizations, tasks related to bank or cash transactions, you should always cross-verify withoutassuming that every-thing will be done perfectly.

Another example would be that your company representative has assured you with a certain profit

Margin on invoice, every time you place order

If you assume that every time the margin % shall remain same, it will not be clever act.

Check with yourself every time whether the margin % remains intact or there are some *invisible* change made in the profit percentage.

Now if you assume and trust everything without checking yourself, you may be deceived now or later.

Better cross-check.

Welfare Priority

This forms part of your *thinking* style.

Many individuals work in an organization starting from the head to the clerk.

There shall be a rule that for the welfare of any one individual, company's welfare can't be sacrificed.

If an individual is given more importance over and above the company, then it ruins the company sooner or later.

If it seems that any individual is getting unfair advantage whether monetary or non-monetary at the cost of the company's welfare, that individual may be shown the exit door.

No individual shall be made greater than the company at any cost and at any point of time.

Rules can't be overruled

This forms part of your *working style.*

Your organisation shall have certain rules to carry on daily tasks.

For a simple example, you have a bicycle shop and you have made a rule for working hours and working days, such as your shop is available from Monday to Saturday from morning 9 AM to evening 7 PM and it remains closed on Sunday.

This is a simple rule which you and your employees has to follow.

Now you found out that one or few of your employees are overruling this rule.

Some are joining the shop by 9:30 AM, 10 AM and 10:30 AM almost every working day.

This is over-ruling or dishonouring the rule.

Now you have some options to correct this.

Option 1 – is to talk with those *late-comers* and ask them to join on time.

Option 2 – slightly change the shop opening time by 9:45 AM

Option 3 – take strict actions by replacing those employees with new ones.

Here again, if you are using option 2, it is overruling the rule. For someone's late coming to the shop, shop's working hours can't be modified.

You may decide for option 1 & 3 which is more convenient to your shop.

Now if you see that your shop gets maximum crowd in the eveninghours after 7 PM and there are idle time in morning hours and this isaffecting your sale.

Then you may decide to extend the evening hours to 9 PM and change the shop hours as 10 AM to 9 PM.

This is not overruling, because it is benefiting your sale and earning more revenue for the shop.

So, the takeaway is Rules may be modified for the sake of the Company but can't be adjusted or changed for the sake of *rule-breaking candidates in thatcompany.*

Is your list ready?

This forms part of your *working style.*

You can solve problems better when your memory is made *free*, when your mind is *free*.

So, how can you do that?

One simple rule is – ***"Don't remember anything, write everything"***

When you write things down in a piece of paper or a note book, your memory gets **big relief** in recalling things, in remembering important things.

You can *anytime* refer to your note-pad and get things completed without any need to try hard in remembering them.

You are here not to memorize or test your memory power.

When your memory is free, then your mind can focus more on finding innovative solutions, to do dynamic things, creative things to address market competition

Now, what is the immediate benefit of this writing habit?

If you build this habit of writing things in front of you, in a small diary or note-pad, which should always be kept open in your desk, then **you will never miss important tasks**, it may get a delay by a day or two, **but it will be under your notice to complete.**

We usually say that **Out of Sight = Out of Mind**.

So when you don't have your tasks for the day *clearly-written* in front of you, then you have to fill your head, your own memory with those tasks.

At the end of the day, you might miss to attend some of them, because human memory has a certain capacity and with age it may decline.

So, you may have to face the consequences when you miss important tasks, phone calls, agendas when you miss them to complete.

SO, NEVER FILL YOUR MEMORY WITH TASKS, WRITE THEM DOWN IN FRONT OF YOU – MAINTAIN A SELF TO-DOLIST DATE WISE.

*(**Imp. Note** - we often commit a mistake to write tha tasks in a diary and close the diary when we get up*

from our desk. Never close the diary, keep it always open infront of you, until you finish ALL of them for that day)

Clarity of Role

This forms part of your *working style.*

When one is not clear about one's role in the working space, then it is more likely that to get unproductive work from that candidate which is not good for the whole organization.

So, one has to be very clear about one's function in the shop or in the organization or in the company.

Once this is clear, then comes contribution assessment.

How he or she is performing on the given role, needs to checked from time to time.

This shall improve quality of performance and contribution to the organization.

Past-Present-Future

Your past was an experience.

Whether good or bad.

Good experiences made your *confidence* stronger, and bad experiences made your *lessons* stronger.

Take lessons and move on.

Your Future is your dreams, your visions, and your wishes which you want to manifest.

Some wishes may get fulfilled some might not. Some may get fulfilled early, some later.

But you shall move on.

And neither past is with you now, nor your future.

What is with you now, is just this moment, right now!

Your present is always with you.

So take lessons from the past, plan for the future and put attention on this present moment for execution.

Because what you did yesterday, had impacted your today. And what you are doing today shall impact your tomorrow.

So do your best today for a better, healthier and brighter tomorrow!

Data is Your Strenght

Data gives you some information.

And Information gives you a direction.

When you get a direction, you implement some action form your side.

Once you implement some action, and it comes out to be fruitful for you, then the Data which you used previously was a *useful* data.

Let's understand this with a simple example in our day-to-day life:-

Let's say you have to travel today to some destination where there is no bus or auto service.

So you have to go by your motor-bike.

Now in the morning you saw that the weather is bit cloudy and you suspect for a chance of *rain & winds.*

So, you checked the mobile application for the weather forcast.

This is an example of data – weather forecast data.

And you saw that on today's date there is a forecast of a rain and winds.

This is an information you received from the weather forecast data.

Now you got a direction whether to travel to your destination today or cancel it.

Due to importance of work you found that you can’t avoid the plan.

So you took rain coat as well as umbrella for the travel.

This is implementation or an action you took to carry your rain-coat jacket with you.

In reality you found out that there was good rain and winds while you were travelling by bike and you were saved from getting wet.

So, the weather data you checked before your travel was a *useful* data for you.

In business, the same rule applies.

There is a lot of data available some are not useful for you and some are useful for you.

Get hold of those data which are valuable to your needs and then take some action.

When you take the right action using the right data at the right time, your chances of winning the competition is more.

How to *Customer*?

Here customer is a noun as well as used as a verb.

"How to Customer" is an art as well as a science.

Some products in certain geography doesn't need selling.

The product sells by *itself*.

For example, there are no sales representatives for gold and diamond showrooms.

Nobody in a reputed jewellery shop will force you to buy their products.

Never.

Because the *subconscious value* of those products in the consumers' mind are very high.

People come, discuss about weight, price, and design. Then decide buy themselves.

Yes, there are guides who tell them which gold ornament has what features and price, weight etc.

In some countries like Singapore, Taiwan, Japan, Thailand, Okinawa, people are highly *health-conscious.*

So, bicycle is considered there as diamond and gold.

People come and buy them, there is no one to encourage them to buy bicycles.

Yes, there are experts who just guide the consumers about the features of the bicycles.

But if you look in India, people are not that *health-conscious.*

So, bicycle has lesser importance to them especially after college or even after school, people tend to use fuel driven vehicles.

Not only for bicycle, for anything to be sold, there is one simple rule –

Customer Attention -> Interest -> Desire to Purchase -> Purchase

First we need to attract the attention from the customer to our product.

This can be possible with our sales skills, experience.

Once we can attract the attention of the consumer, then automatically the customer may get the feeling or interest to try the product or service once.

'Trial Rooms' in garments shop are kept due to this very reason.

When the product satisfies consumer's need, consumer gets the desire to purchase it.

Depending on the financial factors, the consumer finally takes the action to buy that product or avail the service.

This is a very simple process as how a product or service gets sold.

Depending on our skills as to how we can attract consumers' attention, how we can convert a non-cutomer to a customer and make him/her interested for buying the product shall determine our ability to sale.

It is both an art and science to sale any product to any customer or How to make anyone *our customer* for the product or How to *customer?*

Priority Principle

Priority means order or sequence or steps.

When we set the sequence, our mind becomes free of thinking when to do what?

Otherwise we keep planning when to do what, what next, when to do the next, etc.

So, there is a simple rule to set the sequence the tasks depending upon their importance to you and depending upon how immediate that task needs to be done.

Now which tasks are important to you shall depend on your personal lifestyle for the day.

If you are very disciplined and health conscious person, for you keeping a little time for physical excercice, mental hygiene, shall become important or top-most priority.

If your lifestyle is not so, then the same task of physical exercise shall become lesser priority to you.

It is matter of pure personal choice as how we shall live our life and which task we shall give top-most priority or least priority.

As a simple rule we can use this template and prioritize our day-to-day tasks.

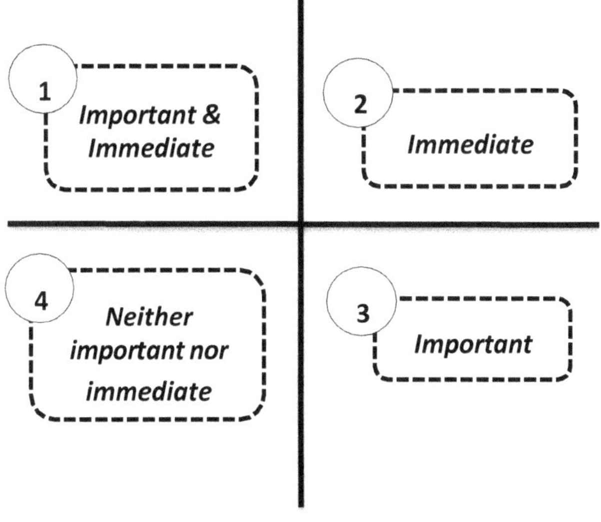

We can clearly see there are 4 segments named in the small boxes.

The ideal practice is to attend and complete tasks in segment (1), followed by tasks under segment (2) and then (3)

Then least priority tasks comes under segment (4) which you may attend later.

When we follow this priority principle then the visible benefit is we shall never miss our commitments our important timelines, which is a boon in our business or profession.

When things get done by the right time, then we have earned a very valuable lesson and discipline in our life that is “Managing Time Judiciously”

Most of us don’t know how timeflies.

Since time is money, but it's invisible.

So when we inculcate this simple habit of prioritizing tasks and then completing them, then we don't have to face any *last moment run & rush* whether in our profession or personal lives.

Money

We all are running behind earning a livelihood rather a glamourous livelihood for a comfortable, happy and a healthy living.

In the process we tend to forget about ideal use of *money*.

As per my understanding we can adapt to 4 ideal principle to use money judiciously and sustainably.

Principle **1**: **MAKE**

It is ofcourse we are making it as per our physical and mental capacity from our profession or business.

Principle **2**: **PROTECT**

It is equally important to protect what we have earned and earning. This makes sure that we can enjoy what we earn now and later.

Bank deposits are a simple example of this principle.

Principle **3**: **BUDGET**

It is true that most of us know the above 2 principles of earning and protecting.

But I have this most of us miss this discipline of ***budgeting.***

To **Budget** means to prioritize the use of money, to prioritize the spending of money.

In middle-class families' especially, we spend money in our personal expenditure, travel, festivities, gifts etc. and never give importance on planning how to save and invest the money for growth.

There is no investment culture taught to children either at school or at home.

We may be expert in bargaining. But that is not saving and growing our money.

Father of investment Mr. Warren Buffet, says that 1st we must plan our earning in saving and investing. What is left over after investment and saving, we may plan for most fruitful expenses for us.

So, ideal budgeting of money shall be using our earnings for saving and investment at the first place.

What is left over after so, shall be used for personal expenses.

Those who can afford, a little portion of our earnings shall also be given in bringing smile and solace to someone *(charity)*.

Gurudev Sri Sri Ravi Shankar Ji (global ambassador of peace and founder of the art of living foundation) says, "at least 3% of what we earn should be kept aside for charity work. This converts the 97% of your earnings into good money"

"Music purifies our mind, Ayurveda purifies our body, seva purifies our action, charity purifies money"

~ Gurudev Sri Sri Ravi Shankar Ji

So, budget your earnings judiciously

Principle **4**: **LEVERAGE**

This is in connection with the *3rd principle* (BUDGETING) that we are working for money day-in and day-out, so is our money working for us?

Is our money being leveraged?

Is our money generating newmoney?

Don't think it to be only FD interest from bank.

Leveraging means making our money work for us fruitfully, making our money grow with time sustainably, making us feel relaxed and collected about our financial strength rather than anxious and tensed about future.

This principle lies in our relation with our earnings, with our money.

Do we have the habit of investing?

Do we know how the share market works?

Do we know how a share of Rs. 10 or Rs. 15 of a company grows to Rs. 700 or Rs. 900 or even more over a period of time?

These questions if arise in our mind, can open the steps towardsleveraging our hard-earned money.

Please don't consider it to be a betting game. As many of us when hear the term "*Share Market*" or "Share Bazar", we immediately associate it to be a fraud market, to be a betting game.

It is not so, in reality.

And it is also not possible for us to keep an eye every moment on the share market news about the rise and fall in share prices.

Here comes the need for a Systematic Investment Plan, SIPs.

There are many mobile applications today where you can invest.

Also there are agents and brokerswho can guide you for investment atthe cost of certain commission.

In case of mobile applications, the investments are free of such commission as there are no middle man.

But for a *new-commer* to this world of investment, initially it is better to listen to some trust-worthy agent or broker.

Later on, one can switch to investing by self through trust-worthy mobile applications.

Whether we do it through agents or apps, we shall built the habit of investing our earnings to grow in future, that is, to get leveraged.

Self-Growth

This is a part of your *thinking style.*

 # *Confidence*

Your Confidence.

Either on yourself

Or

In the profession or business you currently involved.

 # *Presentability*

How do you present yourself in front of customers, in front of dealers, in front of anyone connected with your business or profession?

It's said that the *packaging sales itself.*

The packet, the design, the look of any product is its *silent salesman.*

Any customer first gets attracted by it's look, packaging and design.

Later on, we see what is inside.

But first we get notice of the outer cover only, how it is presented before us.

So, presentability matters for a product as well as for a person like all of us.

Clarity of Communication

For self-growth *clarity of communication* is another essential factor.

Because clarity of communication is a reflection of clarity of your mind.

When you can't communicate clearly, it means there is something not clear in your mind too.

When mind is very clear, your emotions are balanced, your speech can't become obstructed, your communication can't get distorted. It will become clear and smooth.

That is why *meditation* is so important. Clarity of expression and communication is just the by-product of regular meditation.

Those of us practice daily, they can know this fact better.

Clear communication with your colleagues, with customers, withyour seniors and juniors makes you *aman of words, a man of commitment.*(Here women are also included)

When we have all these three,

1. Confidence on either own self or in the profession/business
2. Presentability
3. Clarity of Communication

Then we can climb the ladder for our *self-growth.*

Company & School

If a company can ever be thought a School, then how everything shall look like?

Have we ever thought?

It shall look like the following:-

School Principal = Marketing Head

Teacher = Sales Person

Student = Distributors, Dealers, Retailers

Subject Knowledge = Product Knowledge / Geographical Knowledge

Exam Result = Sales Report

Your Road to Success

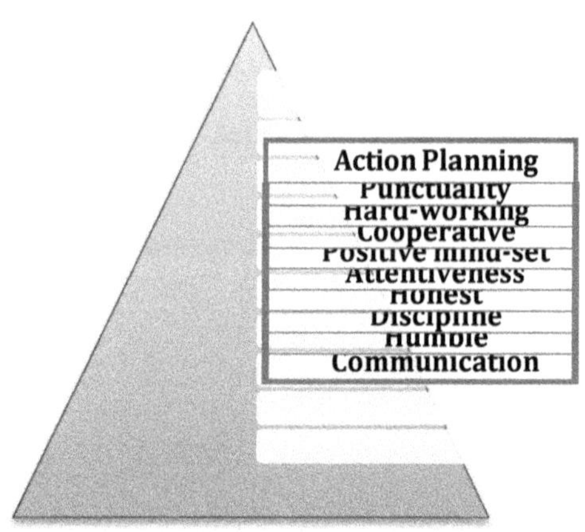

These are based on my observations and my own experience that when you inculcate these qualities in you, your progress is for sure.

It may take some time initially, as we are not used to be disciplined, not used to be hard-working, not used to keep a positive mind-set.

But when we make it a practice everyday, sooner or later all these qualities start manifesting within us.

In fact all these are the different branches of the same tree. When we pull one, others start coming slowly.

For example, when we practice the habit of *planning before doing anything, any task,* then we are in other way becoming disciplined and honest at our work.

Similarly, when we practice culturing a positive mind-sct, thcnthc qualities of attentiveness, clear communication, dedication, automatically follow one after the other.

The decision to be a better atanything begins from YOU!

It also ends with you too!

So, if you decide to change for the better, you shall find ways to do it.

If you don’t decide to do it, you will find many reasons not to do it!

B2B Analysis

While dealing with dealers it quite important to check few of the *key parameters* that might help us in future.

These are few of my observations that we shall look into before appointing any dealer or a channel partner :-

 # Financial Strength

 # Honesty

 # Etiquettes

 # Efficiency

 # Sales Potential

 # Market Share-Revenue *Paradox*

Let's discuss each one of them one by one.

 # Financial Strength

First and foremost we shall see whether the dealer is financially very strong or not?

Whether the dealer shall be able to clear our dues on time or not?

These questions need to get cleared at the first place before appointing a dealer.

 # Honesty

Next comes honesty.

Honesty is to see how the dealer shall be loyal to your company in the future.

Shall the dealer get diverted to *competitive* brands or *competitive* sources of purchases of your brand?

Shall the dealer keep the trust in you in terms of price and schemes?

Shall the dealer honour your dues on time and as per the terms of payment?

How much the dealer can switch over from your product to competitive products or competitive brands?

How much faith does the dealer have on your brand, on your words, on your products, on your pricing, all these are the questions that should be looked into during business tenure?

These are few questions to check while appointing a dealer.

 # Etiquettes

It means how the dealer is well-behaved with you and your people.

A dealer might be very cash-rich but misbehaved, not well-cultured, not well mannered, in communication and expression.

Such dealer may be shown the exit door.

It is very important along with other qualities, that you appoint a well-mannered, well-cultured dealer.

 # Efficiency

Okay now you have a financially strong dealer, well-mannered dealer, who is loyal also.

But the dealer is inefficient.

In this case, none of your work shall get fulfilled on time. Or your *work-procedures* with that dealer may get troubled due to illiteracy or inefficiency of the dealer.

In this case also, you may have to think twice before appointing that dealer. Because you may require *an extra of your person* to help the dealer in executing certain work procedures, which is not affordable in many cases.

Therefore, we have a fair idea that more or less we can think before appointing a dealer.

 # Sales Potential

Before appointing the dealer we need to understand the sales potential of that dealer.

Whether the dealer has some unique potential to attract customers in his shop? Whether the dealer's shop is located in a prime business location or not?

All these shall give us a fair idea whether that dealer has the potential for good sales.

Market Share-Revenue *Paradox*

It's actually a puzzle!

A real-life puzzle in distribution business.

It's only through experience and market knowledge one can bring some balance between Market Share & Revenue.

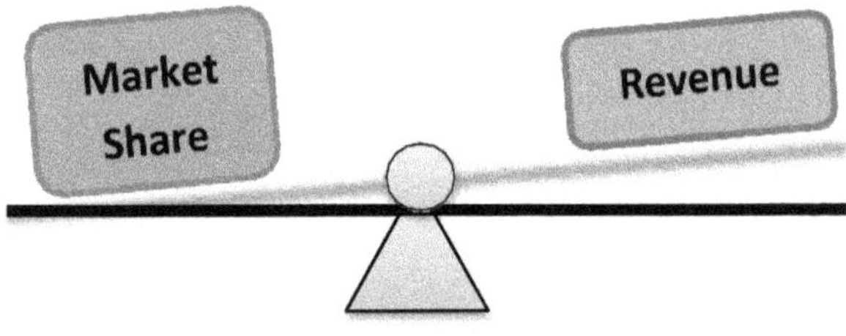

For example there is a dealer who gives you *additional* 10% market share.

But to keep such market share, your revenue needs to be sacrificed by 5-7%

So, it's completely upto you, whether you have profit-maximization motive or market-share maximization motive.

If you have the motive to maximize profit, even if you are okay with less market-share, then you havc to say *good-bye* to the dealer in the above example (who gave you extra 10% market share at the cost of sacrificing 5-7% of your profit margin)

But if you want to lead the market, fight competition, maximize your share in the market, then you may have to skilfully sacrifice some revenue.

Here lies the *paradox.*

Because both revenue and market share can't be increased at the given point of time.

If one increases, the other has to decrease and vice-versa.

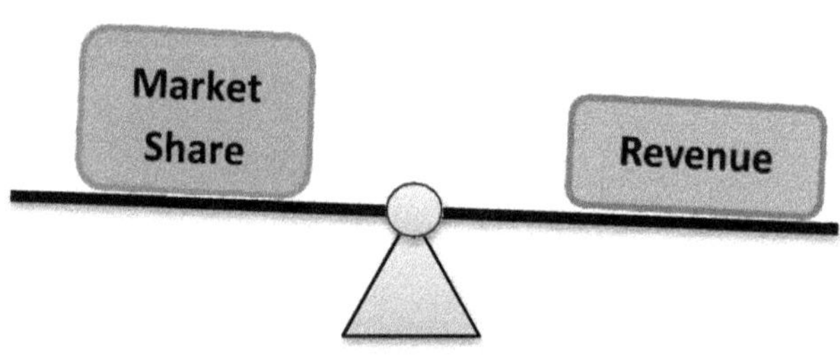

And bringing a parity, a balance between your profit and market share lies the skill!

9 Ideal Practices

These are the list of 9 ideal practices which I have experienced could lead to a better organization which can sail through market competition and even might emerge as a *market leader*.

1. ***Fast Payment & Warm Relation with suppliers***

   When we are honest in clearing dues of oursuppliers, we are in other way writing our name in the *good books* of our suppliers.

   This makes it sure to get support from that supplier as and when we might require in future.

It is quite necessary to keep warm relation with suppliers to get future business advantage.

2. *Fast Service with Proper PDP (Permanent Delivery Plan) to Market*

It is better to have a goods delivery plan.

It is even better to have a *permanent delivery plan* on day to day basis.

Else it may be quite haphazard to deliver the goods to your dealers, in the absesnce of such plan.

It is basically designing the geographical routes of goods supply.

It should ideally mean serving the maximum dealers in minimum travel fuel cost.

3. ***Goods avilability & Range availability***

Availability makes business.

So make it available.

In terms of lumpsum quantity of the one brand or small, small quantities of many different brands.

Choice is upto you. But make it available at the right time.

4. ***Small lot supply with reasonable credit***

Supply lot shall be reasonable.
It need not be huge or gigantic.

A Small lot of supply but a regular basis supply throughout the year can make good business rather than huge lot supply *once upon a blue moon.*

5. ***Door-step service with effective team***

You can't do everything on your own.

You shall need a team.

An effective one.

Who can help you for a door-step delivery of your goods.

Door-step delivery is another feature which can help you to get an edge over other competitors.

6. ***Error free Stock & regular stock reconciliation***

Inventory of goods on your side should be well-maintained.

Better if reconciled daily.

Atleast Weekly, if not daily.

7. ***Crystal Clear Accounting System***

When you keep your books good, you automatically take a sit in the *good-books* of others.

8. ***Good Working Space***

Space makes a sense to us.

You visit a temple. It makes a certain sense to you.

You visit a restaurant. It makes another sense to you.

You visit a clinic. It makes even another sense to you.

Same tiles, same cement, same bricks, same lights.

But *something* is different.

This *something* is the empty space.

It has no colour, yet it can create many different colours in your mind.

It has no voice, yet it tells you many things in your mind.

So, Space speaks!

Creating a good working space does not mean to paste premium quality tiles and marbels and colour & lighting.

Good Working Space means creating a space where individuals working there no more feel *the work* anymore!

People come from office or work very tired, exhausted, dull and tensed.

This is not the sign of a good working space.

People never come exhausted from a park, or a garden, or a sea.

Why?

'Space' is the answer.

Healing Background Music, Meditation, Laughter, Prayer, Group-Lunch, Group-Games, Group-Meditation should be a part of any work-culture.

Playing games is a *therapy!*

When you make two people play a simple game, whether indoor or outdoor, it can slowly wipe-off emotional blockages and communication gaps between them!

You may have noticed when two persons stop communicating with each other, they can never eat together!

They shall feel quite discomfortable to share a tablefor a tea or to share a lunch.

So, when you make them eat together, play together, meditate together, sing together, indulge them in *non-business* matters together, their mind changes, thus their productivity as well.

It may seem to be a eutopian concept, as how can an office arrange such things?

But if this can be applied even for 10-20%. The productivity shall take new heights.

Atleast the working space should contribute positively towards the mental health as well as the physical health of theindividuals.

9. *Working Ambience with mutual undersatnding*

Even if you don't have a luxurious working ambience, but you can build a working ambience where there is mutual understanding amongst individuals.

Creating mutual understanding does not need any monetary cost, but it can return you with a lot of monetary benefit in future.

10. *Cleanliness Is Next to Godliness*

Keep everything clean from your tooth brush to you business files, to your cash-box, to your office table.

Because we all know a common saying, *"Cleanliness is next to Godliness"*.

Self-Reflection

While brushing the teeth in the morning, for the very first time for that day, we look ourselves in front of the mirror.

We look at our face, even we see if there are any scars, pimples or any mark anywhere or not.

Some of us even shave, to look gentle and clean before going to work.

If we can look at our face everyday, can we also look at our own self for sometime during the day?

It's called *self-reflection.*

When we do this even for 2 minutes a day, we get to know where we stand currently, and where we want to go ?

Self-reflection gives you a direction.

Ideally as per my experience we can reflect on the following parameters in our professional lives:-

1. **Quality**
2. **Initiative**
3. **Opportunity**
4. **Fortune**

➢ ***Quality***

Can we reflect on our quality?

Yesterday's me.

Today's me

Same or different?

Better or Not Better?

Yesterday how I managed my work?

Today how am I working?

Is there any improvement in my working style?

Do I wasted less time today than yesterday?

All these are the indication that we are taking a step towards improving our quality.

If we could this, we shall see a positive reflection in our personal and professional careers.

- ***Initiative***

Initiative means absence of lethargy.

When you take initiative, you might not get immediate praise or reward.

But you are sure to get reap the results in the long-run.

- ***Opportunity***

Finding opportunity is a part and parcel of business.

Because best opportunity shall fetch you the best

business, provided you put the best of your efforts.

Also making best use of the current opportunity is also a part of your *self-reflection.*

- ***Fortune***

For some of us it might be a *new* concept.

As there is no physical evidence of *fortune, luck.*

Also there is a common saying that "*Fortune favours the brave*"

But I have a different take on it.

The brave also need the fortune to favour.

There are many examples of unfortunate brave persons in the world.

So you need to understand whether you like it or not, whether you believe it or not, *there is a bigger hand at play.*

When you can shake your hands with *that bigger hand*, then many hands start working in favour of you!

When we honor the divinity in the world and within ourselves, when we pray, when we sing the glories of the divine, go deep within ourselves, meditate for few minutes, we can understand that we are just mere instruments of that divinity, of that *bigger hand.*

So, not only prayer or not only effort.

Both are required.

Self-effort as well as prayer.

"He has no role,

Who has no goal"

~ Sukumar Bera

To Be A Good Sales Person

To sell anything needs both skill and experience.

As per my experience these are the few qualities that makes a sales person a good sales person.

- Sales by Proposition
- Effective Call
- Leadership
- Ownership
- Self-Study or Home Work
- Body Language
- Team Work
- Negotiation
- Self-Competition

Let us explain each one of these qualities one by one, in brief.

Sales by Proposition

It means how you could bring about uniqueness of your product?

What makes you say that your product or service, or whatever you are about to sell, is better than the rest?

How it is better?

What is new in your product/service that differentiates from the rest?

If you can do this, then you are in one way selling by proposition.

Effective Call

This point is connected to the above.

This means ability to make effective sales.

Not only sales.

But *effective* sales.

It means which maximizes your profit or clears your *piled-up* inventory or does both simultaneously.

Leadership

Taking leadership does not mean creating followers.

Leadership means supporting from behind. It is the back-strength.

Because back-strength brings dynamism at the front.

So, leadership means helping each and everyone as and when needed.

Leadership also means absence of *lethargy,* absence of *complaints*.

A good leader shall not involve in pin-pointing others, or highlighting others' mistakes.

Leadership means taking *ownership* and getting things done.

Leadership means finding solution.

Leadership means solving problems or minimizing problems.

It does not mean creating problems or creating excuses.

Ownership

Ownership does not mean position

Ownership means taking leadership.

Ownership means accomplishing tasks in the manner that the *real owner* does not feel the chance to get involved and solve the case.

Self-Study

Self-study here means doing *good home-work.*

It means doing all those things that shall make you a *better you* at tomorrow.

It means absence of *"will-see-tomorrow"* – attitude.

It is only through your good home-work, you shall reap the fruits in your professional arena in future.

Body Language

Keeping a *learning attitude* is good enough.

Even if you don't utter any word, your *body-language* thousands of words about you!

Your body-language is your silent speaker.

So, speak well!

Team Work

One-Man-Show had never been successful in any venture all over the world.

So, you shall need a helping hands, infact many such helping hands who shares common motive like you.

When you have a strong team, a like-minded team, half of your job is done. Because your team shares half of your effort in achieving the goal.

Negotiation

For a good sales man, negotiation is an inherent quality.

Negotiation is different from bargaining.

Negotiation brings a *win-win-win* state.

Win for you, Win for your Company and Win for the party standing on the other side.

Bargaining shall bring *Win-Loss* state.

Self-Competition

When you compete with yourself, you won't develop jealously, hatred, tension and worries.

When you compete with yourself, you get better everyday.

When your days get better, your month has to get better and so your year!

So, you should have 2 competitors in your mind.

Yesterday's YOU

Vs.

Today's YOU

If you have the above 2 competitors in your mind, your mind shall be free of fears, insecurity complex.

But if you have competitors like

YOU

Vs.

Others

Then you can think of a host of negative tendencies taking a sit in your mind and ruin your enthusiasm.

Because your productivity depends on your *state of mind*, on your *quality* of your mind.

Any success is first won at the level of mind, and then on the ground.

So keep your competition only with yourself, learn from others' mistakes, never compete with others.

Factors Affecting *Counter-Share*

There are many factors that affect Counter Share.

Counter share means how much your counter or your shop holds a share in the total sales of all related counters or shops in a given geography within a given time frame.

For example, in the year 2022-23 in Midnapore Region there are 20 Sweet Shops.

Total Sales in Value in that Year in that region was suppose 10 Lacs.

Let's say you also have a sweet counter in Minapore which sold sweets worth 2 lacs in 2022-23.

So your counter-share = 2 lacs / 10 lacs = 20%.

This counter-share depends on several factors.

As per my experience it can broadly be categorized into two factors.

1. **Operational Strategy**

2. **Marketing Strategy**

Operational Strategy

- *Rational credit,*
- *Availability & Service,*
- *Profitability*

Rational credit

In case you work on credit, take reasonable credit depending on your level of business.

Working on smaller and mini-credit throughout the year is better than taking huge credit one time and feeling the heat of clearing the dues either through bank-loan or own-fund.

Availability & Service

Make the products available in your shop, in your counter.

In case of depending solely on one single brand, try to keep a good variation of different products of the same brands as well as different brands.

Profitability

Also consider your profitability. Try to convince your customers in buying high profit products from your shop, also slow-moving items.

Marketing Strategy

- *Visibility*
- *Product Mixing*
- *Branding*

Visibility

That which is made visible sells more than that which is not.

Prime Location of your shop and Prime Display of your products are quite responsible for sales of your product.

Product Mixing

Keep a good mix of products, mixed brands, mixed items of same brands, Products with different price levels.

Product mixing helps you to cater to a wide array of customers who have a wide array of tastes, preferences, choices.

Branding

Although you might be selling goods of different brands, you should create a ***brand*** of your own.

It does not mean to bring literally create a new brand with new company name of your own.

Here creating a ***brand*** **of your own** means creating a different space in customers' mind about you, about your shop, about your service, about your approach towards customers.

For example there are two sweet shops selling more or less same variety of sweets.

Sweet **Shop-A** gets less customer visits throughout the year.

Sweet **Shop-B** remains always busy with customers.

Why?

Same sweets, same raw materials, same sweet packets.

But why customers prefer to buy from Shop-B more than A.

Because Shop-B has created a brand of its own.

Shop-B uses hand cover and spoons to serve sweets. The shop boys uses hair-caps while serving sweets. The shop temperature and ambience is kept cool and decent, so that a hungry customer can relax well while eating. Shop-B has good lighting to showcase all sweets properly. Shop-B has put insect repellent machine to avoid insects to enter the shop and distrurb the sweets.

All these factors has made the customers to think that **Shop-B** is the most decent and hygienic sweet shop to buy from.

This is the *unique branding* that **Shop-B** has created of its own, although both Shop-A & B areselling the same sweets.

In the same manner, you can create a different identity of your shop in the eyes of customers, even if your competitors are selling the same products.

This the value of ***branding***.

Qualities of Worker

I have seen different people who work for the company, with the company.

Some of them grow financially over time, and some do not.

Some rises the ladder, some goes down the ladder, and some are out of the ladder.

So, as per my experience there are broadly 4 catgories of people who have different working styles.

It is only their style of working that determines the qualityof their work.

Let's see who these 4 categories of people or 4 categories of worker are.

1. Working Style = Normal or Routine 9-5 Job Worker is *Good.*

2. Disciplined Worker is *better*.

3. Value Addition worker is *best*.

4. Quality Improving Worker is *Extra-Ordinary*.

3rd category of people rise the ladder of growth faster, followed by 4th and 2nd category.

When someone adds a positive value to the company whether financially or physically, then the company grows by that.

And when company grows, then that person's growth is a by-product.

4th category person is the most valuable asset for any organization.

As he/she does not stop his/her learning process.

When ***learning process*** is **ON**, then quality improvement is a by-product

And when there is improvement in quality, there ought to be addition of some value, which makes the 4th type of worker extra-ordinary :))

Employee Behaviour

There are two important factors that determines *Employee Behaviour*

First is **Relation**.

Second is **Task.**

Relation means how old the employee is to the company.

Here relation does not mean *personal relationship* with some physical person.

Here relation means how close the employee is to the company. How he/she is close to the day-to-day affairs of the company.

Task here means what is meant to be done, the responsibilities of that employee.

Now there can be 4 situations of an employee's mind-set.

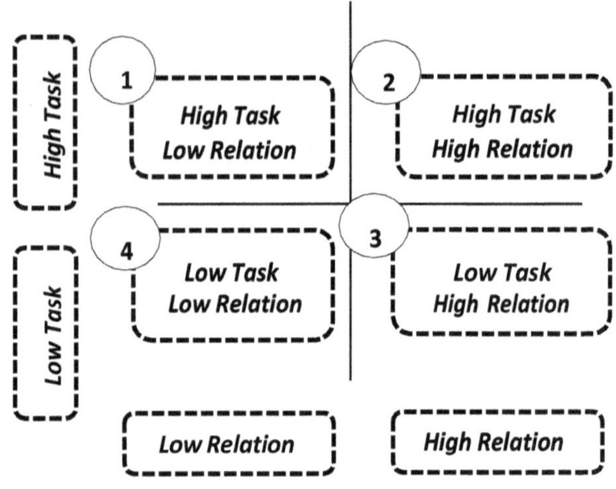

LT-LR *(Low Task - Low Relation)*: When Employee Joins the Company, He/She works on **instruction.**

Next is (High Task – Low Relation) HT-LR, where the employee, works on a little **motivation**, in case the person feels motivated due to either monetary reasons or non-monetary reasons such as office ambience, work-life balance, social status, family etc.

Next is *(High Task – High Relation)* HT-HR where the employee works without any need for micro-management, there is **automation** in work, also there is a possibility of *(Low Task – High Relation)* LT-HR where the employee may be shown the ***exit-door***, as the company does not get any value-addition from that employee.

Working Mentality

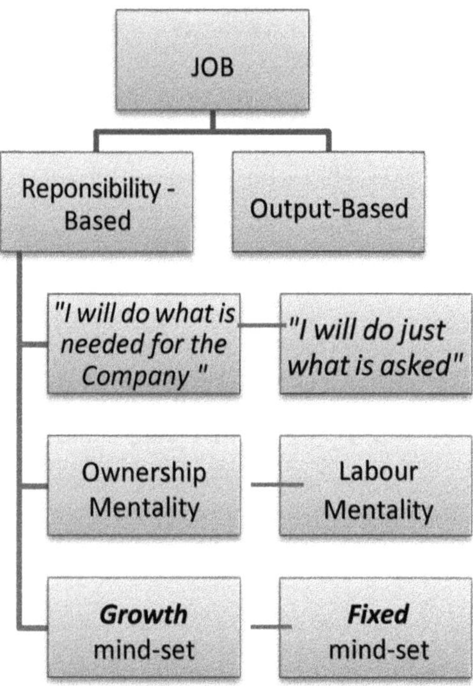

AOA-Mix

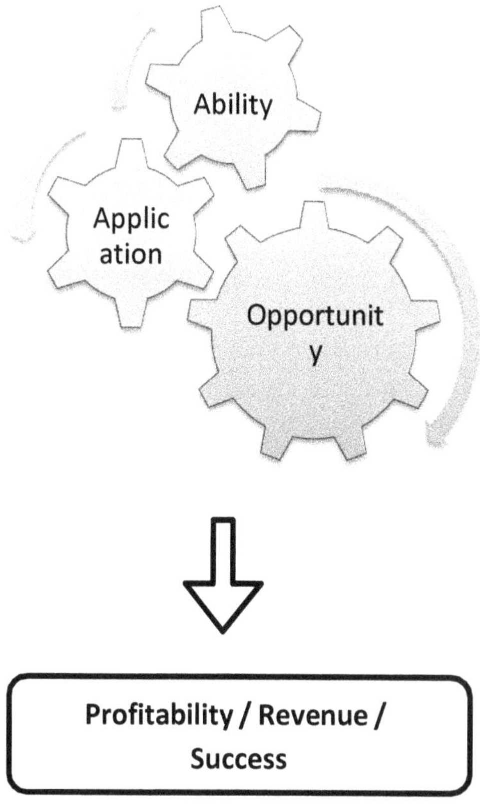

Ability corresponds to sales team's ability.

Opportunity corresponds to market and product and Application corresponds to the business organization.

A perfect mix of ability, opportunity and application will increase the chances for success.

"explore passion, then set ambition"

~Sukumar Bera

Market Size & Market Share Matrix

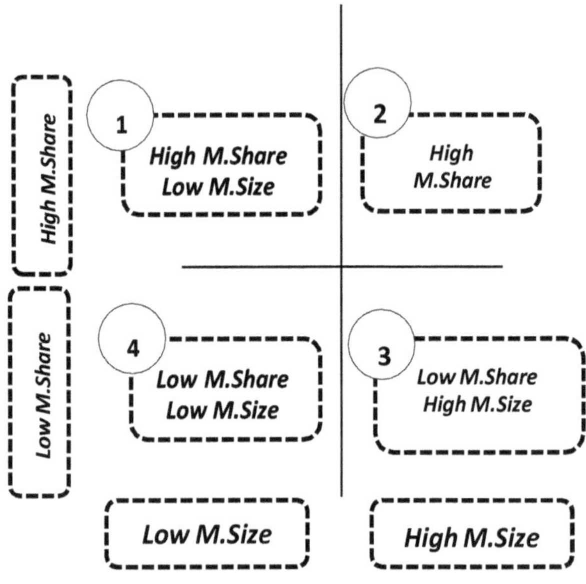

Here **Market-Size** refers to the total market potential or total-sales potential for the particular product during a given period of time.

Here **Market-Share** means how much percentage your sales have in the total *Market-Size.*

We can see in the *4-by-4 matrix* above that there can 4 situations possible.

Now, our focus is to see when to do what. What action we can take at what situation for profit-maximization or loss-minimization.

When the market size is low or small and you have high market share in that market size, then **you should focus on *Customer Service.***

Excellency at customer service can fetch you good results and profitability.

Similarly, when the market size is very small and so your share in it. It is intelligent to exit or discontinue for you to minimize losses.

When there is HMS (high market size) and HMSH (high market share) the **Customer Relation, Placement of Full Range, exclusive showroom all these shall help.**

When you see that Market Size is Huge but you have a low market share (that is HMS-LMSH), then **Price-Penetration, Branding, Innovation** all these shall help.

Revenge or Progress ?

Prefer One.

So, when we prefer revenge.

Two things are possible.

We may win or we may lose.

Our winning shall leave a fear of future revenge from the other side.

Our losing shall leave us with the feeling that we are weak and meek.

So, decision to revenge *is not a winning at all*. In both cases we shall have to suffer.

But when we prefer **personal growth, we are always on the winning side.**

Because when we focus on our progress, we are eventually

becoming strong. And when we become so strong, your competition with others dissolves, as *anybody* shall think twice to compete with you!

Revenge is a **Fixed Mentality.**

Progress is a **Growth Mentality.**

To Bounce Back

Even if you couldn't make upto your expectation or you could not succeed.

Never Mind!

You always have one thing in your hand, fresh and untouched.

That is *your future.*

Your future always remains undisturbed and fresh.

Your future is your possibility for progress.

So, if you have the confidence, after every set-back, bounce-back.

And when you want to bounce-back

When you have the confidence you can create everything that you desire.

So at the phase when you want to bounce-back to success, *check the following parameters:-*

1. **Quality than Before**
2. **Revenue before Budget**

Quality Than Before means checking the level of quality. Have you

To let customers buy your things, have you improved the quality of your things than before?

Is anything made to enhance the quality of your product?

If so made, then sales shall show up, and so your profit, making you come slowly to your desired position, after bounce back.

Next is **Revenue before Budget**.

It means *spreading you leg lesser than your blanket.*

Check your revenue first, then decide for making an expense or purchase.

When we keep revenue in mind before budgeting then you are on the safe side, your organization is on the safe side.

If we neglect our revenue while deciding for incurring an expense, that might eat-out reserve and capital, which is *not-at-all* a healthy sign for the organization to bounce back.

Skills to Achieve Target

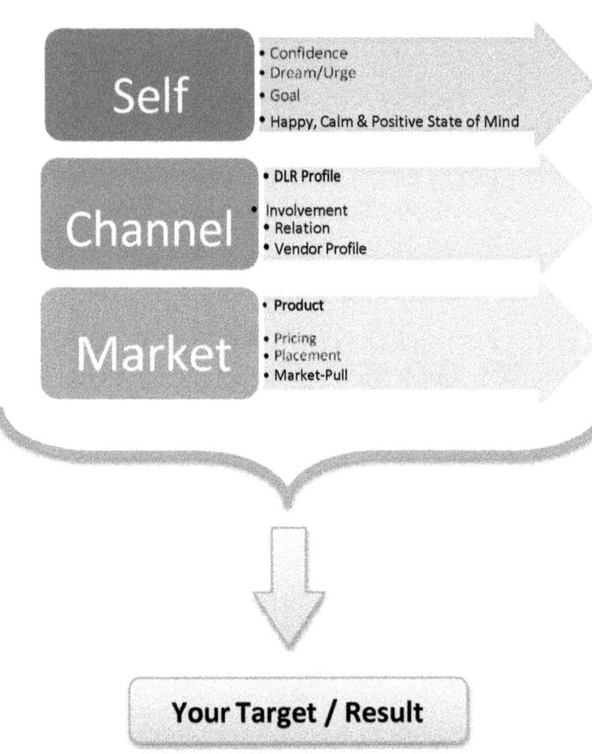

Types of People

Best-People = Give Good Memories,

Better-People = Give Company,

Good-people = Give Happiness,

Bad-People = Gives you bad expereinces,

Worst-People = Leaves you with good or best lessons.

Existing Resource & Diversification

There is another puzzle for us in this world of managing business.

Stay or Expand?

Continue the old or add a new?

Existing Resource or Diversification?

As per my observation many have taken not so correct step in diversifying as by doing so, the exisiting resource was disturbed.

Diversification is a possibility when the existing resource is not disturbed, even if your involvement is divided.

When you plan for diversification, it is quite obvious that a portion your involvement shall accrue to this *new venture*.

Now if you can make it sure that whether your involve more on this *new venture* and less on the existing venture, your old-existing resource does not get disturbed, then you are okay to sail to the new-venture.

When you see that your non-involvement or less involvement in the exisiting venture for the *new venture* is affecting your existing resource in the long-run then this diversification is not a good idea.

Automation is a key here.

Buiness Automation.

It means your business does not get affected whether you sit in your office desk or not.

Whether you get involve or don't, your business performance and team work doesn't get much affected. It can work hassle-free.

If this system can be developed then you are said to have *automation* in your business.

Now this not a One-day task.

You need to develop technical competence in your people, training, inspiring, problem-solving skills and working spirit and technological support for you to have automation.

Only technology can't create automation. People and technology and Working Mind-set of People together create automation.

When you can create a successful business automation, then diversification might be a possibility.

If not, then not.

Categories of Dealers

For any distribution company it is quite obvious to deal with a wide array of its customers, its dealers.

In the course of such dealing, I have found out that dealers can be categorized broadly in 2 parameters.

Although dealers can be categorized into many different parameters as well but the sake of simplicity, I have taken only 2 parameters which we all can easily relate to.

These are :-

1. **Finance**
2. **Attitude or Approach**

Here *finance* means the financial strength of the dealers, how fast or correctly they clear your dues.

Attitude or Approch means the behaviour of that dealer, how professional he/she is?

Writing, Speaking, Talking and overall behaviour or attitude of the dealer constitutes – *Attitude or Approach.*

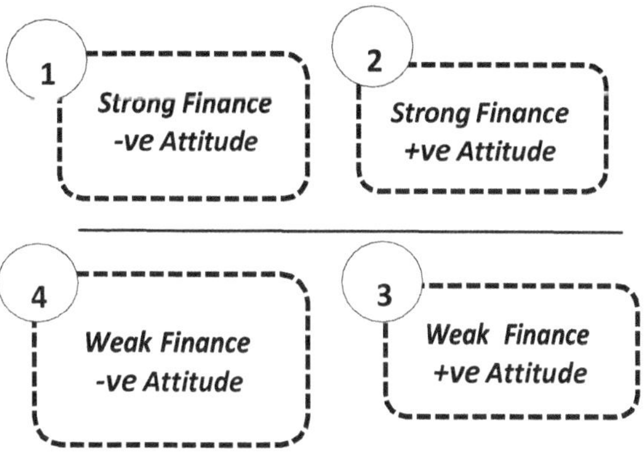

This forms part of your own working and thinking style as which dealer you shall entertain and which you shall not.

There is no fixed rule for this.

So, there can't be fixed steps for a distributor as how to deal with its dealers.

The *4-by4 matrix* drawn above can give a fair idea as broadly what can be done for a particular category of dealers.

For instance, dealers in segment 4 who have weak financial strength and also have a **–ve** attitude, such category of dealers may not fetch you much growth near or future. So, they might take a sit in your black list.

Now, it is your own philosophy as how to treat other category of dealers. There is no such clear and specific maths for this.

This a dynamic and customized game.

It is possible that a dealer has **–ve** attitude but you might have to entertain them for they shall fetchyou *more milk* in the long-run.

So, being not so rigid or stringent on anything helps us to adjust as per circumstances.

Allowing a bit of *flexiblility* is the key.

The Most Important Person In The World!

We attend meetings. Greet executives, meet company heads, national heads. Attend speeches from great personalities. We exchange experiences, learn from people.

In doing all these, we seldom attend to the most important person in the world, who can make us or break us.

No seminars, talks, strategies can work when this most important person is not given attention.

This is that much person of importance whose smile, wellness and happiness worth the whole planet and beyond.

Nothing in this world, whether business or non-business can equate with compromising happiness and *well-being* of this person.

If we learn to manage *this person*, behave well with *this person*, then business or profession shall be managed well too.

Because whether business or profession, everythings starts with *this person* and completes with *this person* too.

So, who is *this person?*

This person appears to us everytime we stand in front of the mirror.

This person is none other than your own self.

YOU are the most important person in the world.

It does not mean being selfish for oneself.

It simply means nothing in this world can be compromised for the well-being and happiness of oneself.

When you can manage yourself well, then managing other things is not that tough.

When YOU are not an issue, then other issues do not seem big.

When YOU are strong, happy and healthy, keeping others' happiness and wellness is not tough.

When YOU don't have any problem, then solving external problems seem not so big.

When YOU are joyful, making others joyful is possible.

Now, just imagine the reverse.

When YOU are an issue yourself, how can you solve other issues of your world.

When YOU are not well, what well-being you can create for others?

When YOU are not happy from inside, what Happiness you can spread to others?

When YOU are not well-managed, how can you manage anything?

YOU are the centre of everything around you.

Whether its business or profession, when you give enough attention to your self for health, happiness and strength, when you can manage your mind well, then you shall find managing other things is happening effortlessly.

It is often said, that *"When You Can Win Over Your Mind, You can Win Over the Whole World"*

So, when we can manage ourselves better, manage our mind better, managing the external affairs in the world – whether business or profession shall get managed better.

We often hear the term *Time Managent.*

In reality, it's a vauge term.

Nobody can manage time. Time manages us, in fact. We are bound by time and space from nature. How can we manage time.

Impossible!

Rather the correct phrase is Mind Management. When we manage our mind well, our emotions well, our thought process well, **the time** gets automatically managed effortlessly.

When we manage people and events, the **time** gets automaticallymanaged.

SO, if we feel to attend to our world better, we shall first have to learn to attend to ***this most important person*** better.

Attending to this person means, ***Taking responsibility for our own body, mind and emotions.***

As we take ownership and responsibility for our business and profession, we similarly have to take responsibility and ownership for our own body and mind and its ***holistic well-being.***

www.ingramcontent.com/pod-product-compliance
Lightning Source LLC
LaVergne TN
LVHW021156160826
845679LV00024B/2140

* 9 7 9 8 8 9 6 1 0 4 9 7 1 *